# STATIONS OF DESIRE

MICHAEL A. SELLS

# STATIONS OF DESIRE

LOVE ELEGIES FROM IBN 'ARABI AND NEW POEMS

"Amazing! How could it be that the one pierced through the heart by love had any remainder of self left to be bewildered? Love's character is to be all consuming. It numbs the senses, drives away intellect, astonishes thoughts, and sends off the one in love with the others who are gone. Where is bewilderment and who is left to be bewildered?"

—*The Young Woman at the Ka'ba*

ISBN 965-90125-1-9

IBIS EDITIONS
POB 8074
German Colony
Jerusalem
Israel

*To Janet*

# TABLE OF CONTENTS

# TRANSLATOR'S NOTE

I HAVE ATTEMPTED to keep the transliteration of Arabic terms in what follows as simple as possible. In the introduction, I have not used diacritical marks with names or words that have an accepted anglicized form such as Muhammad, Qur'an. For other names and terms, I have used diacriticals when the name is first introduced, but dropped the diacriticals thereafter. Thus readers will encounter Laylā, Ghaylān, Ḥimā, and *nasīb* followed thereafter by Layla, Ghaylan, Hima, and nasib. In the translations, I have marked the Arabic terms with a stress accent to indicate how they would be pronounced in an anglicized form within a stress system: Láyla, Ghaylán, Híma. In the glossary I have used both forms, allowing those not familiar with Arabic to fit the transliterations to an approximate English pronunciation. When referring to turjuman as the guide, I use roman type. When referring to it as the title of Ibn 'Arabi's collection of love poems, I use italics. In the table of contents, the selections are numbered according to their order in the Arabic text.

Many have contributed to these translations and poems. In particular, I wish to acknowledge Ed Allderdice, Etel Adnan, Luce López Baralt, Amila Buturovic, Pablo Beneito, Jane Carroll, Jane Clark, Aaron Cass, Peter Cole, Granville Collins, Doug and Susan Davis, Simon Fattal, John Felstiner, Seemi Bushra Ghazi, Sam Goldberger, Jerry Gollub, Mike Haxby, Regan Heiserman, Stephen and Sara Hirtenstein, Maggie Hivnor, Emil Homerin, Rachel Krauser, Denise Levertov, Paul Losensky, Janet Marcus, María Rosa Menocal, Ariela Marcus-Sells, Maya Marcus-Sells, John Mercer, Pat Michaelson, Paul Nagy, Martin Notcutt, David Oldfather, Ruth Ost, Aida Premilovac, Frances and Christopher Ryan, Raymond Scheindlin, Harold Schimmel, Layla Shamash, Jaroslav and Suzanne Stetkevych, Bob Townsend, Richard and Cecilia Twinch, and Alison and Nick Yiangou. Special thanks to all the *udaba* of the Muhyiddin Ibn 'Arabi Society.

# INTRODUCTION

*Riders along stations are we, fated to arrive*
*And to depart,*

*With such long hopes spun over*
*Such short lives.*[1]

—al-Buḥturī

IF WE TRAVEL TO EGYPT, we are likely to encounter a young man who will ask if we need a turjumān (a guide, or translator) to show us the sites:  tombs of the Pharaohs, mausoleums of the Mamluks, a lost city in the desert, or catacombs with mysterious symbols carved into the walls.

But there is another kind of turjuman in the Middle East: the love poet.  When we enter the Arabic love poems of Ibn ʿArabi, for example, we find a turjuman who will show us the rock ruins of the ancient Nabataean city of Hājir in the Arabian desert, the city that the Qur'an tells us was destroyed by a great scream after its people had slaughtered the sacred camel mare of God—a city of the same Nabataean people as Petra, that "red rose city half as old as time." He might then show us the meadow sanctuary of the bedouin known as al-Himā; the rocky area of La'la' (Stone-Flash) associated with lightning and with the promise of rain and the life it brings; 'Udhayb with its bubbling spring of waters "as cool as life"; or Zamzam, the sacred spring at Mecca, visited by pilgrims with its waters of healing and blessing.

Some of these sites are the abandoned camps of the beloved. They are the stations (*maqāmāt, manāzil*) of her journey away.[2] At the beginning of the expedition, the turjuman will stop at the ruins of a particular campsite, some marks made by tent poles in the sand, burned rocks used for cooking, the remains of a trench used to keep out rainfloods. There in the midst of the strange and desolate, a recognition occurs. These are not just any ruins; they are the traces of the one we know. As these strange marks in the sand configure themselves into the traces of the beloved, the poem is born.

The moment in which we recognize the traces leads to remembrance *(dhikr).* We remember the last time we saw her. We remember when the wasteland around us bloomed from spring rains. We remember her disappearing into the embroidered coverings of her camel palanquin or howdah *(howdaj)* along with the other women of her tribe and slowly disappearing into the distance, until the palanquin could no longer be distinguished from the tamarisk trees or boulders.

As she moves away from us in space and time, we recall and name her stations. We remember them, one by one. Or do we imagine them? After all, the beloved is distant from us and yet, somehow, the turjuman allows us to follow her journey. We ask the East wind—the messenger between lovers—about her. We ask the stations through which the beloved passed. The stations and the ruins they hold do not respond. Or when they do respond, their words wound.

Sometimes a phantom of the beloved appears. (The ancient word for phantom of the beloved is *khayāl,* which becomes the word for imagination.) She may speak to us. We ask her why she left. She argues it was not her choice. She grieves. We grieve. We forgive her. In some cases it may not be clear to whom we are speaking exactly: the beloved in person or the East wind, the voice of the ruins, the phantom—all of whom may speak on her behalf or carry her message.[3]

The effort to track after the beloved can cause madness. Qays—better known as Majnūn Laylā (mad for Layla)—wanders from station to station looking for Layla. He thins away just as the camel-mare thins away on the long desert journey. He loses his wits. He talks to the animals. He addresses the trees as Layla. He addresses the rocks as Layla. Qays is crazed, or as the etymology of the name Majnun suggests, *jinned*—taken over by those desert genies who are the muses of the Arabian poem, the semi-spirits of love and madness.

According to legend, Majnun Layla lived at the time of Muhammad, haunting the dried-out river valleys (wadis) of Arabia. The poems attributed to him and the legend surrounding him have epitomized the notion of the poet-lover as a martyr to love. Majnun's life is finite, his longing infinite. It is little wonder then that Sufis, those Islamic mystics wandering in the infinite reaches in search of the one they love, have also taken him as a model. When the mystic lover is thinned away and broken down, when he can no longer hold on to his self or his thoughts, when he is emptied of his own words and arguments, the beloved reveals herself.

For Majnun, this is the moment of love-madness. For the Sufis in general and Ibn 'Arabi in particular, love-madness is analogous to the mystical bewilderment (ḥayra) that occurs as the normal boundaries of identity, reason, and will are melted. The self of the lover passes away. In this "annihilation" (fanā') he becomes one with the divine beloved. In a famous hadith, Allah proclaims: "When I love my servant, I become the hearing with which he hears, the seeing with which he sees, the hands with which he touches, the feet with which he walks, the tongue with which he speaks."[4]

But for a Sufi and poet like Ibn 'Arabi, such a passing away and union with the beloved, though eternal, is also—within our world of space and time—ephemeral. It is a valid manifestation of the real (al-ḥaqq). But it cannot be possessed. To try to keep the image of the beloved known in the union is to freeze it into an idol. The worship of such frozen idols, which are constructed as "gods of belief" within theologies, philosophies, and religions, leads to a world of mutual intolerance. Each person or group worships the god of one belief and denies the god of the other. For Ibn

'Arabi, who sees the divine beloved as both transcending the world and immanent within every manifestation, such denial is a form of unbelief (*kufr*). The only true affirmation of oneness is the affirmation of the one reality in each of its manifestions along with the refusal to confine it to any one of them. One whose "heart is open to every form" would need not simply to tolerate the manifestations of reality in each belief, but to actively appreciate them.

Ibn 'Arabi frequently quotes the Qur'anic verse to the effect that in each moment Allah "is in a different condition" (Q 55:29). Nothing infinite can be kept in a place or time or image. The lover and the mystic must have a heart that is open to every form. Even the religions, theologies, philosophies, and other systems of thought that Ibn 'Arabi knew so deeply are only stations along the path, or constantly shifting forms of that which transcends fixed determinations. In the philosophical context, this notion of the heart receptive to every form is a mordant critique of dogmatisms of all kinds and a call for a life of openness to new understanding. In the context of love poetry, the heart in perpetual transformation reflects the shifting of the beloved's manifestations and personae. In *Translator of*

*Desires,* the context of love poetry is most apparent, although certain verses come close to explicit intersection with the theological expression:

Pasture between breastbones
and innards.
Marvel,
a garden among the flames!

My heart can take on
any form:
for gazelles, a meadow
a cloister for monks,

For the idols, sacred ground,
Ká'ba for the circling pilgrim,
the tables of the Toráh,
the scrolls of the Qur'án.

I profess the religion of love;
wherever its caravan turns
along the way, that is the belief,
the faith I keep.

Like Bishr,
Hind and her sister,
love-mad Qays and his lost Láyla,
Máyya and her lover Ghaylán.

from "Gentle Now, Doves"

Here, the heart open to every form is receptive to the different manifestations of beauty and the different systems of belief. The last verse of the poem offers the famous lovers of the poetic tradition as examples of those who entered into the bewilderment that is caused by such openness.

For Ibn 'Arabi, she whom we love is beyond the world, but within everything. Her forms are ever changing. And although the feminine gender of the beloved is inherited from the classical tradition, Ibn 'Arabi is particularly bold in his willingness to figure the deity as a female beloved, as in the poem "Armies of My Patience" (poem 2, below).

Elsewhere Ibn 'Arabi expresses the notion of perpetual dynamism through a play on the Sufi context of the "moment" (*waqt*). In terms of mystical love, the moment is the experience of union with the beloved.

Some people, Ibn 'Arabi says, have one moment in a lifetime: they encounter reality, seize it and hold on to it for the rest of their lives. Others have a moment every year; they are able to give up attachment to the old form and be open for the new every year. Some have a moment every month. Those who have a moment every month miss the weeks. Those who have a moment every week miss the days. Those who have a moment every day miss the hours. Those with the hours miss the minutes. The goal is to have a moment of one breath: with every breath to give up attachment to the old manifestation and be open for the new. This transformation leads to bewilderment and love-madness. Thus the poet-lovers who perished in the forms of their beloved are cited in the verses quoted above as examples. Similarly, in every moment the Sufi "passes away" only to return or remain in the next moment shaped around the new form. For one with a heart that can take on every form (*qābil li kulli ṣūra*), each new moment brings both loss and joy.

Sufis extended the original meaning of condition or state (*ḥāl*) beyond the momentary mood or attitude of the beloved toward the lover. They also extended the meaning of the station (*maqām*) beyond the beloved's journey away from the poet and beyond the pilgrimage. For Sufis a state could occur without personal control, while a station was more stable and entailed a certain intentionality in entering into it and attempting to perfect it. Thus, for example, the station of poverty might last until the Sufi had arrived at progressive levels of poverty, culminating with the reliquishing of poverty itself as a possession. The states (such as absence and presence, separation and union, intoxication and sobriety) come over a person in rapid succession and without warning (just as the beloved's mood can shift without any warning to the lover).

Beyond such Sufi categories of states and stations, another world of stations can be found in the various levels of Muhammad's journey through the heavens and the Sufi journeys through the heavenly spheres that were modeled on those of Muhammad. Thus Ibn 'Arabi refers several times in his love poems to the station of Idris, the Qur'anic prophet associated with the Biblical Enoch and the Greek Hermes. The station of Idris is a celestial station, part of a seven-tiered set of passages from the earth through the heavens. The mention of the station of Idris would bring to mind the story of Muhammad's night journey and ascent (*mi'rāj*) to the divine throne. Also associated with this mythical world of cosmic ascent is the station of Bilqīs, the queen of Sheba. Bilqis, bewildered by the polished tiles of Solomon's palace, thought she was standing in water and lifted her skirts. A similar mistake can be made by the Merkavah mystics at the divine throne who are counseled not to shout "water, water!" when they gaze on the tessellated tiles and fear they are drowning.[5] The association of Bilqis with Idris reflects a theme in the heavenly ascent that was shared by Jewish, Christian, Muslim, Harranian, and other Near Eastern mystics. When the voyager arrives at the divine throne and sees the reflections, he becomes bewildered. What image appears in those reflections: deity, angel, devil, or human? At this phase, at the threshold of mystical union, any mistake can be fatal.

Finally, Ibn 'Arabi's life journey itself can be broken into stations: through Andalus (Murcia, Seville, Cordoba); North Africa (especially Fez and Tunis) and Egypt; the Arabian holy cities of Mecca and Medina; the eastern Mediterranean (Konya, Baghdad, Aleppo), and finally Damascus. These stations are within the realm of historical observation, but they are no less mythic in autobiographical comments by Ibn

'Arabi and in hagiographies of his commentators. Love poets like Ibn 'Arabi charted a dual topography. They journeyed through the stations of the lovers of the classical tradition. At the same time they moved through the stations of ritual pilgrimage and devotion. The wit of the poetry as well as the autobiography is found in the weaving together of these two symbolic worlds.

\*

Muhyiddīn Ibn al-'Arabī was born in 1165 near Murcia, Andalus. His father, a military official in the Emir's court at Seville, traced his lineage back to ancient Yemen. Leading the life of a highly educated member of the civil service, Ibn 'Arabi looked forward to a career within the Almohad administration. But he chose a different way: *siyāḥa* (wandering). After becoming a Sufi, Ibn 'Arabi set forth on a lifelong journey. He travelled through the villages, towns, and cities of Andalus, with important stays in Seville and Cordoba. He experienced his formative mystical visions in the North African cultural centers of Fez, Marrakesh, and Tunis. He went on to Cairo, to Mecca and continued to travel throughout the eastern lands—Damascus, Aleppo,

Baghdad, Mosul, Konya. Finally, Ibn 'Arabi settled in Damascus, where he died in 1240 of the common era, 638 of the Islamic era. His tomb there has become a popular Sufi shrine, and today Ibn 'Arabi is known as the grand master (ash-Shaykh al-Akbar) of Islamic mysticism.

Midway through his journey, in Mecca, he composed his collection of love poems, the *Turjumān al-Ashwāq* (The Translator of Desires, The Guide to Desires, or The Translation of Desires).[6] He calls these poems *qaṣīdas*, after the classical pre-Islamic qasida (ode), although they differ from the classical qasida in tone and emphasis. The pre-Islamic qasida was composed of three, relatively independent sections: the remembrance of the beloved (*nasīb*), the journey or quest, and the final boast. After the nasib, the poet would set off on a journey through the desert, alone, by camel-mare, confronting the heat of the day, the terror of the night, hunger, exhaustion, mortality, and fate. In the pre-Islamic qasida, there was always a strict distinction between the journey of the beloved away from the poet, the *ẓa'n* (which always occurred in the nasib), and the journey of the poet/lover (which occurred in the second section of the qasida). The poet's quest or journey would end with him returning to his tribe and boasting of the tribal values of generosity and heroism, and the poem would conclude with either a personal boast or the praise of a tribal prince.

Ibn 'Arabi's poems are qasidas in the sense that they contain elements of the poet's journey and of his boast, but these elements are always subsumed within the nasib. His journey is never a journey away from the beloved to an integration into a world without her, but always a circling back after her. Thus the poet/lover follows that path of the beloved and incorporates her original stations into his own pilgrimage. This change in the interior trajectory of the qasida began with the Majnun Layla, whose legend can be traced back to the time of Muhammad, but whose historicity and provenance remain shrouded in controversy and mystery. The love-mad Majnun would and could never break from the remembrance of the beloved. The poems attributed to Majnun made the nasib an independent poem on its own, a love poem or ghazal.

In addition to the ghazals of Majnun and others who composed in this style (known as the 'udharī school), another ghazal tradition, more light-hearted and erotic, also grew out of the nasib at the time of

Muhammad. The ghazals of 'Umar ibn Abī Rabī'a, the most famous member of this school, constitute for Ibn 'Arabi a continual source of allusion. In 'Umar's poetry, the stress is on the erotic quest of the lovers, their efforts to elude watching family members and surpass other obstacles, their sexual banter, their attempts to achieve a secret rendezvous and the occasional success. Another feature of 'Umar's ghazal, amply reflected with Ibn 'Arabi, is the fatal face of beauty. The lover is slain by the arrows of the beloved's eyes, struck by the lightning flash of her teeth, targeted by the bow of her eyebrows.

To Majnun and 'Umar we must add the third major love poet in the early tradition of the Ummayad period: Ghaylān, also known as Dhū al-Rumma ("The One with a Rope Cord").[7] Ghaylan specialized in the the nasib-qasida. Like Majnun and 'Umar, Ghaylan specialized in love verse. Unlike them, however, he kept the full structure of the classical qasida, even as he subsumed the journey and boast into the poetics of the nasib. As in the later qasidas of Ibn 'Arabi, Ghaylan's journeys were circular, tracking back in search of his beloved, Mayya. Like 'Umar, Ghaylan's poems contain dialogues or traces of dialogue between the poet and beloved. Unlike the dialogues in the ghazals of 'Umar, however, the dialogues of Ghaylan are ghostly dialogues, between the lover and the phantom of the beloved, or the memory of her.

In his preface to this volume of nasib-qasidas or ghazal-qasidas, Ibn 'Arabi dedicated the poems to Niẓām, the daughter of a Meccan shaykh and the niece of a famous shaykha (female scholar) with whom Ibn 'Arabi had hoped to study. Nizam's beauty, Ibn 'Arabi tells us, was overpowering—beyond direct description. The etymology of her name is based on a root $n/ẓ/m$ that has meanings of "beauty," "artful arrangement," "perfected harmony," and "fluency." Such beauty was commonly compared to the stringing of pearls. A lover of puns, Ibn 'Arabi at one point proclaims that in seeking Nizam he has become "undone and unstrung." The order and harmony, as connoted by the words based on $n/ẓ/m$, apply to expressive composition, as in poetry and the Qur'an, making Nizam a figure for both poetic inspiration and divine manifestation.

In his preface, Ibn 'Arabi recalls a strange encounter at the Ka'ba. As he was performing the circumambulation, he recited a love poem (poem 1 in this volume), thinking he was alone. A young woman touched him softly on the back and began to question each verse. Concerning the final verse, on bewilderment, she protested that love is all-consuming; a true lover would have no self left to be bewildered. Ibn 'Arabi suggests that her challenge led him to compose the rest of his work. In the philosophy of Ibn 'Arabi, the mysterious woman (assumed by most scholars to be Nizam) speaks from the perspective of the lover in time and space, in constant oscillation between annihilation in love and remaining within the world. In the tension between the two perspectives, she becomes a force that draws the poetry to continually renewed intensity.

After he was criticized for writing erotic poetry unbefitting a Sufi shaykh, Ibn 'Arabi composed a new preface that left out the earlier dedication to Nizam and stressed instead the allegorical meanings of his poems, meanings he announced he was expanding upon in his own commentary, which would link an allegorical reading of the erotic elements of the poetry to various aspects of his wider thought. Ibn 'Arabi wrote more than two hundred books, one of which, the *Meccan Openings,* is currently being issued in a new Arabic edition of more than thirty volumes. Into these works he incorporates every aspect of Islamic learning (philosophy, theology, alchemy, astrology, law, grammar, logic, literary criticism, moral psychology, and Sufi psychology). If the critics were to refute his allegorical interpretations, they would have had to engage the entire system. Their outrage over the sensuality of his love lyrics was not, apparently, enough to motivate them to master the larger, interconnected universe of his writings, a mastery prerequisite to the condemnation of any single work.

The commentaries of Ibn 'Arabi take up a wide range of theological issues within a prose enriched by the metaphors and themes of the poetry. They offer useful bridges to his metaphysics.[8] Yet by focusing almost exclusively on mystical theology, the commentaries pass over in silence other areas of meaning—such as the deep and constant allusions from the classical Arabic poetic tradition within the poems, and even the way in which Ibn 'Arabi further incorporates into the tradition of love poetry the rituals and language of Islam.

Ibn 'Arabi's commentary is silent on other important symbols as well. Thus, in explaining the word Nāmūs, which appears in poem 2, below, Ibn 'Arabi glosses it as simply "the good" (al-khayr), without commenting on its meanings of law (from the Greek nomos) and of spirit, great spirit, Gabriel, or paraclete (from the religious literature).

To privilege Ibn 'Arabi's own commentaries in reading the poems is to ignore the danger of the intentional fallacy, the Platonic and Qur'anic point that poets are often unable to intepret what they say, and Ibn 'Arabi's own philosophy that any commentary or interpretation can only provide a fleeting glimpse of the meaning.

The love-elegies of the Turjumān al-Ashwāq have been neglected by modern scholars—in part because of the artificial division in modern Arabist scholarship between religion and poetry. Specialists in Arabic poetry have shied away from the Turjuman because they accepted at face value the suggestion that the poems were nothing but purely mechanical, Sufiizing allegories for metaphysics. Indeed, I have found little discussion of the *Turjuman* as poetry. On the other hand, students of Ibn 'Arabi's metaphysics tended to avoid the *Turjuman* precisely because the connection to the mystical theology in the poetry itself was not transparent. Ibn 'Arabi's commentaries on his poems make certain selected aspects of his metaphysics clear. But if they were to be taken as the full meaning of the poems, they would render the poems themselves superfluous.

Such is indeed the fate of any poetry when it is read through an allegorizing interpretation based on one-to-one correspondences between poetic image and theological concept. We moderns continue to have difficulty in understanding the medieval Arabic cultural world in which an erotic ghazal could be appreciated on either level or both with complete enthusiasm and sincerity. This difficulty is compounded by the valid concern within Sufism as a practice to make sure that the erotic energy unleashed through the use of meditational *dhikr*, poetry, and music does not overwhelm the powerful shaykh–disciple relationship and lead to abuse, or that Sufis who recited erotic poetry not be accused of socially scandalous behavior.

Yet, like most Sufi poets who are read beyond the

circles of their immediate schools, Ibn 'Arabi had a commitment to the lyrical mode. It is worth noting that, toward the end of his life, when Ibn 'Arabi was conscious of passing on his legacy to his school of disciples in Damascus, he made the reading of the *Turjuman al-Ashwaq* a regular part of his sessions and it is the *Turjuman* that Ibn 'Arabi, of all his works, chose to recite in person, rather than having one of his students recite it.[9]

In the translation of desires, there is no end to the argument over whether the beloved is human or divine. As the beloved in Hafiz's ghazal said: "Don't ask, this story is so long it is beyond telling."[10] Some things are clear about her, however. She is constantly moving from station to station. She appears harsh, tender, faithful, and fickle as she transforms herself through various states *(ahwāl)*. She suddenly shatters into the plural and we speak of her as "them." "She" can become "he" within a single poem. Or, the feminine can be used to refer to a male beloved, or the male pronoun to a female beloved. In whatever form we try to seize her, she eludes us. She cannot be possessed. To attempt to possess her and seize her in a particular image is more than idolatry. The desire for possession violates the *adab,* the basic politesse of how love works. (Adab is so central to the intricate patterns and obligations of behavior that it also came to mean "literature".)

Ibn 'Arabi had stated that the poems of the *Turjuman* were inspired by his Hajj. However, he complicates the identification with the Hajj through his intensive evocation of the stations of classical Arabic love-poetry. And when Ibn 'Arabi mentions the stations of the Hajj, he often interiorizes them. Thus, in referring to Minā, the Hajj station where pilgrims ritually cast stones (representing their egoistic tendencies) away from themselves and where the great sacrifice in remembrance of Abraham occurs, Ibn 'Arabi writes:

Never may I forget that day
    at the stoning grounds at Mína,
at the fields of sacrifice,  at the spring of Zámzam—
    and what transpired there.


        Their stoning ground, my heart
      May they cast their pebbles there!
        their field of the sacrifice, my soul,
    their sacred spring, my blood.

The poetic station and the religious ritual, the outer and the inner, the subjective and the objective are inverted, entangled, and ensnared just as the "lords of love" in the first poem of the collection. The stations are sometimes personified and speak. They can be desolate and silent. The relationship of journeyer to journey can be reversed; the voyager—the lover—remaining stationary as the stations themselves perform a circumambulation or ritual encircling of the lover. Ultimately, Ibn 'Arabi tells us, the mystic reaches the station of no-station, open to all forms of the beloved, possessing none.

In addition to the allusions from the classical poetic tradition, the poems in the *Turjuman* offer a number of terms and symbols particular to Ibn 'Arabi. For example, the camels of the beloved that lead her from station to station are the *'is*, the red roans. There were thousands of epithets for camel in classical Arabic poetry, and the poet could choose among the epithets to continually renew and expand upon the effects of the camel image. In addition to its evoking of a sandy or red roan coloring, the word *'is* allows Ibn 'Arabi to make multiple puns on the word for Jesus, 'Isa (sometimes anglicized as Eissa)—the prophet with whom Ibn 'Arabi claimed a particularly close, personal relationship. The rules of word combination mean that the two words become perfect homonyms, and Ibn 'Arabi can shout to the camel-driver, "don't lead the *'is(a)* (a)way!" and evoke both the camels that bear away the beloved and Ibn 'Arabi's special prophet at the same time.

Also peculiar to these poems is the importance of the statuette goddesses, the *dumā*. These were evidently small, white alabaster figurines with red streaks that were used in Syrian Christianity. For Ibn 'Arabi, they became a fascination. While some would view any such figurine as an idol, for Ibn 'Arabi all reality reflects the one God, and reflects it on every level from spirit, to animal, vegetative, and mineral. Thus the stone reflects an aspect of that deity, the aspect that is deeply silent before the entreaties and the questions of the lover.[11] As with other major poets influenced by Sufism, Ibn 'Arabi played upon the issue of idolatry, reversing expectations, and focusing the problem of true idolatry not on figures of this or that religion, but on the "gods of belief" that become the centers for exclusivism and intolerance.

*

The title of Ibn 'Arabi's most famous collection of poems, *Turjuman of Desires (Turjuman al-Ashwaq)*, that is, Guide, Interpreter, Translator, or Translation of Desires, raises the enigma of translation. For Ibn 'Arabi, translation is no word-for-word mechanistic rendition from one system into another. It is a simultaneous process of "bringing across" and transformation. In every moment, the heart must change to receive the new form of the constantly changing beloved.

An early meaning of the English "translation" and Latin *translatio* is the ritualized transport of relics from one shrine to a proposed new shrine. The new shrine or holy place is not sanctified until the relics arrive. In Ibn 'Arabi's poems, when the beloved and her company pass through a station, they both inhabit it and enliven it. When they leave, it is desolate. When the poet-persona recognizes the traces of the beloved in the ruins of a campsite, the memory of the beloved possesses the poet. When the memory is lost, the poet, like the ruins in their emptiness, is laid waste. Similarly, in Ibn 'Arabi's philosophy, when a state of consciousness passes through a person, it takes over that person completely, and when it leaves, it leaves the person empty until a new state of consciousness arrives.

If translation is not a word-for-word rendition of a static image, but an attempt to reflect the transformations of the beloved in every new form and gesture, then the boundary between translation and creation is no longer very clear. In the process of translating Ibn 'Arabi's *Translator of Desires* I also composed original poems, a few of which are included in this volume. When I felt I was unable to bring alive in translation the beauty of the original, I would find myself composing poems of my own. In the process of composing poetry, I would be led back into Ibn 'Arabi's poems with a new perspective. The translations presented here represent a little more than one third of Ibn 'Arabi's *Translator of Desires*. I have numbered them in the table of contents according to their place in the Arabic original, and have given them titles. As was the custom in Arabic poetry, Ibn 'Arabi presents his poems without titles with the expectation that the reader or listener would remember the poem by its first line, end-rhyme, and meter. For readers not steeped in the original Arabic, titles offer compensation for the more traditional method of orientation.

Classical Arabic meter is based on quantitatively

long and short syllables or variations of syllables. A vowel can be long by nature or position (followed by two consonants). Depending upon the meter, the metrical foot can have three, four, or five syllables or variations of syllables. Each verse is made up of two half verses or hemistiches with a final end rhyme or assonance.

Ibn 'Arabi composed the majority of his poems in seven of the more common classical meters. It is not possible for the translator to reduplicate in natural English verse either the intricate metrical patterns or the complex end rhymes. Yet it is vital to find an analogue or means of compensation for the effect created by the rhythm and sound of the original, especially the rhythmic tension between the syntax and the meter. I have used the tension between syntax and line breaks as the prime analogue to the original Arabic rhythmic tension. In both the Arabic original and the English translation, there is a play between tension (when the syntax is cut by meter or line break) and release (when the pauses of syntax align with meter of line break). In order to utilize the line break in this way, I have divided a single Arabic verse into four English lines, although I have used other line formations when they were more appropriate to the mood and tone of the original. To compensate for acoustic features such as rhyme and assonance, I have employed alliteration, half-rhymes, and various forms of acoustic parallelism.

While grounded in the traditions of classical Arabic poetry and its integration into the Islamic world, these poems are often stunningly original. Thus, while Sufis frequently used the love poem to represent the deity in the feminine, poem 2 ("Armies of My Patience") is one of the most brilliant and extended treatments of God in feminine form ever composed in an Abrahamic tradition.

The plays upon Islamic religion and love are also numerous. Poem 14, for example, is an extended play upon the category of hadith, the traditions of the prophet Muhammad. But the isnād—the chain of authorities going back to the original speaker—is like none other. And this is the only hadith I know of where the receiver of the message sends a response back through the chain of authorities to the original speaker.

These poems can be read with the finest love poems of the Middle Eastern tradition, the same tradition that, through the Arabic poets of Spain, influenced the troubadours. This is also the tradition that stretches from the oldest Majnun Layla poems to the Layla of Eric Clapton (which was inspired by the English bluesman's encounter with the Nizami version of Majnun Layla in a London bookshop).[12] As high literature the poems of the *Turjuman* embrace and bring to life centuries of classical Arabic poetic tradition. As love lyrics they are also as straight-to-the heart as a song played on the street corner.

*Haverford, Pennsylvania*
*11/9/99*

NOTES

1. Jaroslav Stetkevych, *The Zephyrs of Najd: The Poetics of Nostalgia in the Classical Arabic Nasib* (Chicago: University of Chicago Press, 1994), p. 85, poem 28.

2. Following on the pre-Islamic Arabic tradition, the beloved is most often figured as female and the lover as male. Although Ibn 'Arabi and other later poets will sometimes refer to the beloved with the male pronoun as well, the ancient bedouin motif carries a formal gender marking not only through the female names used for the beloved and the feminine grammatical constructions but also through rituals and customs of a gender-marked bedouin society, such as the use of howdahs by women. Many Andalusi poets lack the neoclassicist emphasis on ancient bedouin love poetry that is found with Ibn 'Arabi and thus

a less gender-marked, sometimes gender-ambiguous, at other times openly homoerotic, lover–beloved construction is possible. In what follows, I use the feminine in referring to the beloved and the masculine in referring to the poet-lover persona as a reflections of the particular bedouinizing poetics found in Ibn 'Arabi's *Turjuman*.

3.   For the phantom in ancient Arabic poetry, see John Seybold, "The Earliest Demon Lover:  The Tayf al-Khayal in the Mufaddaliyat," in S. Stetkevych, editor, *Reorientations: Arabic and Persian Poetry* (Bloomington:  Indiana University Press, 1994), pp. 180-89.

4.   For an account of Ibn al-Farid, the Arabic poet who brought the stations of pilgrimage, of love, and of mystical experience together most strongly, see Th. Emil Homerin, *From Arab Poet to Muslim Saint:  Ibn al-Farid, His Verse, and His Shrine* (Columbia: University of South Carolina Press, 1994).

5.   For a full discussion, see the first half of David J. Halperin, *Faces of the Chariot: Early Jewish Responses to Ezekiel's Vision* (Tubingen: J.C.B. Mohr, 1988).

6.   The translations below are based upon the following editions: Ibn 'Arabi, *Tarjuman al-Ashwaq* (Beirut: Dar Sadir, 1966); Ibn 'Arabi, *Dhakhā'ir al-A'lāq: Sharḥ Turjuman al-Ashwaq*, ed. M. al-Kurdi, which includes the full commentary of Ibn 'Arabi on his poems; and  Ibn 'Arabi, *The Tarjuman al-Ashwaq:  A Collection of Mystical Odes*, trans. and ed. Reynold Nicholson (London: Royal Asiatic Society, 1911), which includes Nicholson's translation along with the Arabic text.  A fine new translation of the full poems and commentary has recently appeared:  *Ibn al-'Arabi, L'interprète des désires (Turjuman al-ashwaq)*, translated by Maurice Gloton (Paris: Albin Michel, 1996).  For biographies of Ibn 'Arabi, see Claude Addas, *The Search for the Red Sulphur* (Cambridge: Islamic Texts Society, 1993) and Stephen Hirtenstein, *The Unlimited Mercifier* (Oxford: Anqa Publishing and Ashland: White Cloud Press, 1999).

7.   For a discussion and translation of one of Ghaylan's

qasidas, see Michael Sells, *Desert Tracings: Six Classic Arabian Odes* (Middletown: Wesleyan University Press, 1989).

8. Elsewhere I offer an extended discussion of the relationship of these poems to Ibn 'Arabi's mystical theology, particularly his theory of the heart that is receptive of every form: M. Sells, *Mystical Languages of Unsaying* (Chicago: University of Chicago Press, 1994), chapters 3 and 4.

9. See Gerald Elmore, "Sadr al-Din al-Qunawi's Personal Study-List of Books by Ibn al-'Arabi," *Journal of Near Eastern Studies* 56.3 (1997): 161-181, especially pp. 175 and 179.

10. See Ghazal 42 in *The Green Sea of Heaven, Fifty Ghazals from the Diwan of Hafiz*, translated by Elizabeth T. Gray, Jr. (Ashland: White Cloud Press, 1995). In addition to Gray's version of Hafiz, a number of excellent new translations of Middle Eastern poetry have recently appeared. See *Ottoman Lyric Poetry: An Anthology*, translated by Walter G. Andrews, Najaat Black, and Mehmet Kalpakli (Austin: University of Texas Press, 1997); *Wine, Women, and Death: Medieval Hebrew Poems on the Good Life*, compiled and translated by Raymond Scheindlin (Philadelphia: Jewish Publication Society, 1986), *Selected Poems of Shmuel HaNagid*, translated by Peter Cole (Princeton: Princeton University Press, 1996), and *Poems of Arab Andalusia*, translated by Cola Franzen from the Spanish translations of Emilio Garcia Gomez (San Francisco: City Lights, 1989).

11. I have refrained from adding extensive notes to this collection. Elsewhere I have written on these poems, the poetic and mystical traditions out of which they spring. See M. Sells, "Ibn 'Arabi's Gentle Now, Doves," *The Journal of the Muhyiddin Ibn 'Arabi Society* 10 (1991): 9-11; idem, "Longing, Belonging, and Pilgrimage in Ibn 'Arabi's Translation of Desires," in Ross Brann, ed., *Languages of Power in Islamic Spain* (Ithaca: CDL Press, 1997), pp. 178-96.

12. For a rich discussion of the relationship of love poetry and the vernacular, see María Rosa Menocal, *Shards of Love* (Durham: Duke University Press, 1994).

# LORDS OF LOVE

## TRANSLATIONS FROM IBN 'ARABI'S
### TRANSLATOR OF DESIRES

LORDS OF LOVE

I wish I knew if they knew
    whose heart they have taken

Or my heart knew
    which high-ridge track they follow.

Do you picture them safe
    or do you picture them perished?

The lords of love in love
    are ensnared, bewildered.

## ARMIES OF MY PATIENCE

The day they left
they saddled their red-roan camels
only to carry peacocks
    on them.

She takes possession
with a glance that kills,
like the Shéban queen
    Bilqís on her throne of pearl.

When she walks
on the tiles of polished glass,
you see a sun on a sphere
    in the stone of Idrís.

What her glance kills
her speech revives,
bringing the dead to life,
    like Eissa.

Her Torah—the tables
of her legs in splendor.
I follow after her
        and study, like Músa.

Bishopess daughter of Byzantium,
unadorned,
the light you see on her,
        Namús.

Wild one, solitary,
she takes for retreat
a mausoleum,
        to remember.

The sages of our tradition
she dumbfounded,
Davidian psalmists, rabbis,
        and priests.

A hint from her
she wished the gospel

and just like that! you'd think us priests,
patriarchal highnesses in flowing robes.

The day they left me
I set loose squadrons,
squadrons along the path,
        the armies of my patience.

As my soul rose to my throat
I begged that beauty,
that grace:
        Save me.

She relented.
God shielded from us her fury.
Salvation's angel
        drives Iblís away.

As they saddled her camel
mare for departure, I cried:
driver of the red roans,
        don't take the Eis' away!

## THEIR STONING GROUND MY HEART

Two friends,
    turn aside at al-Kathíb,
and pull off the track at Láʻlaʻ,
    seeking the waters of Yalámlami.

      You will find there
      those you came to know.
      Theirs are my fastings,
      my pilgrimages, my festivals.

May I never forget a day,
    at the stoning grounds at Mína,
at the fields of sacrifice, at the spring of Zámzam,
    what happened!

      Their stoning ground, my heart,
      may they cast their pebbles there!
      their field of sacrifice, my soul,
      their sacred spring, my blood.

Camel-driver, when you
        come to Hájir,
stop the camels there for a time,
        give greetings,

                And call out toward the red
                pavilions of al-Híma
                        salutations of a lover
                longing for them, lost.

If they greet you back
        wish them peace and bless them.
If they are silent
        leave them and journey on

                To the river of Eissa
                where their camels were unbridled,
                        white tents nestled
                along the mouth of the stream.

Call out to Da'd and Rabáb,
        Záynab and Hind,
Sálma and Lúbna,

then listen.

Then ask is there at Hálba
a girl who shows you
    the radiance
of the sun when she smiles?

## AS NIGHT LET ITS CURTAINS DOWN IN FOLDS

Peace, Sálma, and peace
to those who halt awhile
at al-Híma. It is right
for one like me to greet you.

Would it have hurt her
to return the greeting?
Ah, but a statuette
goddess is beyond control.

They left as night
let its curtains down in folds.
I told them of a lover
strange and lost,

Surrounded by yearnings,
struck by their arrows
on target always,
wherever he goes.

She smiled, showing her side teeth.
Lightning flashed.
I couldn't tell which of the two
split the darkness.

Isn't it enough she said
I am in his heart
where each moment he sees me,
isn't it, no?

## HEARTBREAK SOUGHT THE PLAIN

Yearning sought the highlands.
Heartbreak sought the plain.
I was trapped somewhere in between
Najd and Tihám,

Contraries
that can never join.
Undone, unstrung,
I will never find Nizám.

What can I do, what
is the plan? Guide me,
scold! Don't
rattle me with blame.

Sighs ascend
to the highest spheres
of the heavens, as tears
stream down beneath my eyes.

The red roans yearned
for lush, watered meadows,
returning home on tender feet,
the yearning of the lost.

After them, I live
only to pass away.
Good-bye to her then,
patience, good-bye.

## AMID THE SCENT OF ABSINTHE AND MORINGA

Our treasured friends are gone
    and with them our patience,
        gone who had been alive
    in the black core of the heart.

I asked where the riders halted
    and knelt their camels.
        Amid the scent of absinthe,
    they said, and moringa blossoms.

I told the wind to
    track them down
        in the shade of the thicket
    where the wings of their tents were spread,

To bring them greetings
    from the brother of grief.
        When the tribe scattered,
    his heart was torn.

IN GOWNS OF DARKNESS


As I touched the stone
    I was jostled by ladies
circling the Ká'ba
    with veiled faces.

They lowered their veils
    revealing the sun in glory.
They warned me
    death is in the gaze.

We've left many men dead
    at Muhássab in Mína,
souls come questing
    to the mound of stones,

In the courtyard of the wadi,
    on the high ridge monuments
of Ráma and Jam',
    among the crowd that throngs the 'Arafat plain.

Don't you see beauty
    plunders a heart that's pure?
Beauty, virtue's spoiler,
    aptly named.

Meet us at the Zámzam spring,
    after the circumambulation,
near the middle tent,
    near the boulders,

There a man thinned away
    by the trance of love
is cured by the scent of the women
    that made him yearn.

When disquieted
    they loosen their hair
and let it fall
    enfolding themselves in gowns of darkness.

## IN MEMORY OF THOSE WHO MELT THE SOUL FOREVER

Their spring meadows
are desolate now.  Still, desire
for them lives always
in our heart, never dying.

These are their ruins.
These are the tears
in memory of those
who melt the soul forever.

I called out, following after
love-dazed:
You so full with beauty,
I've nothing!

I rubbed my face in the dust,
laid low by the fever of love.
By the privilege of the right of desire for you
don't shatter the heart

Of a man drowned in his words,
burned alive
in sorrow.
Nothing can save him now.

> You want a fire?
> Take it easy.  This passion
> is incandescent.  Touch it.
> It will light your own.

WINDING LIKE SNAKES


Lightning flashed for us
        in Abraqáyn.
Thunder clashed
        between our ribs.

The clouds let down a fine rain
        over sand-slipped hills,
over quivering branches
        bending toward you.

The stream banks burst
        amid a rush of fragrance.
Doves sent out their cry,
        the green sprigs tender.

They tied down the red tents
        between rivers
winding like snakes.
        Among them

Demoiselles, radiant
        as suns rising,
dark-eyed graces,
        understanding, tender.

## IN THE MIRROR OF A MAN

She said: I wondered at a love
that struts its glory
through the garden's
    flowers as they blossom.

I said: don't wonder
at what you see.
You see yourself
    in the mirror of a man.

## GENTLE NOW, DOVES

Gentle now, doves of the thornberry
and moringa thicket,
don't add to my heartache
your sighs.

Gentle now,
or your sad cooing
will reveal the love I hide,
the sorrow I hide away.

I echo back, in the evening,
in the morning, echo,
the longing of a love-sick lover,
the moaning of the lost.

In a grove of Gháda,
spirits wrestled,
bending the limbs down over me,
passing me away.

They brought yearning,
breaking of the heart,
and other new twists of pain,
putting me through it.

Who is there for me in Jám',
and the Stoning-Ground at Mína,
who for me at Tamarisk Grove,
or at the way-station of Na'mán?

Hour by hour
they circle my heart
in rapture, in love-ache,
and touch my pillars with a kiss.

As the best of creation
circled the Ká'ba,
which reason with its proofs
called unworthy.

He kissed the stones there—
and he was entrusted with the word!
What is the house of stone
compared to a man or woman?

They swore, how often!
they'd never change—piling up vows.
She who dyes herself red with henna
is faithless.

A white-blazed gazelle
is an amazing sight,
red-dye signaling,
eyelids hinting,

Pasture between breastbone
and innards.
Marvel,
a garden among the flames!

My heart can take on
any form:

for gazelles a meadow,
a cloister for monks,

For the idols, sacred ground,
Ka'ba for the circling pilgrim,
the tables of the Toráh,
the scrolls of the Qur'án.

I profess the religion of love.
Wherever its caravan turns
along the way, that is the belief,
the faith I keep.

Like Bishr,
Hind and her sister,
love-mad Qays and the lost Láyla,
Máyya and her lover Ghaylán.

# BETWEEN THE MUSIC AND THE GRAVES

POEMS BY MICHAEL A. SELLS

ORISHA

Will you bear these voices
They find you out and are saying

they are your tongue
bluesback echoes of longing

the man on the bass played by the gods
the man on the bass played by the earth

in the audience some talking
above the song, some broken, some sly, some gone

some hear and are enfolded

When you dance
someone might recognize your step

doesn't matter if you think you're worthy

which spirit takes you chosen
breaks you down
and liquefies
molten ore of gold or silver flowing
like water she walks upon the air
like water she walks upon the earth

only an intimation in the gait
giving her away

The train rolls from the market slowly,
people gentle, as if they knew.

Bazaar around the bend
not there before,
items retrieved and revealed.
How to find in the world
of the worn, lived-in, for resale,
beneath the arches and vaults,
those who cannot see.

> Beneath the verandahs,
> violet in the dust and haze,
> you walk, too slow—
> how to pass the intersection
> of music and graves.

Out of order sign on the station wall.
Land of the dispossessed and free.

Ruins of civilizations on ruins of towns
on ruins of villages on ruins of camps of those who
    wander.

From a distance, the call of the stations,
each name fading in the soft night air.

Unusually kind, they know me better
than I, memory of her my blood.
There is still time, before
the effect wears off.  The car
clicks along the rails and sways.
No reason to move ever.
You've given yourself away.

Abandoned tires along the tracks,
patches of scrub willow,
graffiti.

I was here.

NO ECHO

The first to pass, after leaving town
are the orchards at the edge of the mountain.
Darkness falls, blue, then violet, then black
on rows of trees.  No one has seen it
fall this way before.

From the switchback ridge
the rock-face drops into darkness.
No echo.  Bones
glow from the cliff wall cave
without flame.

Something for you in that
broken town, walls bleached
and split in the sun,
like torn cardboard,
like weeds grasping down,
open to the sky beneath you
without tongues. You look

where it was before.
Someone in the family
knows, isn't saying.

Where were the waterfalls?
Wrong turn where the tire ruts scatter,
pine shadows closing.

Who brought you then?
Who was whispering in the spray
and roar, something you knew
receding beneath recall.

AVATAR STREET

In the soft air
between dusk and dark
children take over the lawns.

Plaster peeling
on the second floor,
a notebook page, handwriting
too neat to have been yours.
Always smaller than it seemed.

How'd she die? they ask.
Careful not to walk
on the sidewalk lines.

Late afternoon, thistle
        purple, buried
in the high grass, rusted
        machines. Wrenches
don't match much

of anything anymore.

Main street in decline,
Accident, you say, don't
know why. Avatar Street.
Down on her luck,
wrong part of town.
A house is burning.

Chain link at
the end of the road.
Renovation underway.
Go back one more
time. Take something.

It all seems smaller
than it used to be.
Porch rails cool
the hands. Bricks
glow red sapphire.
Inside, the living
room is as

it was before,
nothing changed.

She turns back
toward you with
a look of surprise.
Can't stay. The car
is waiting.

## DESCARTES MEDITERRANEAN

I.
Sunset here is like
no other.  Down both sides,
palaces and pensiones flash
their fusillade. Bridges
double in a mirror of calm.
Arches hold an exploding
sky, gold in fire, streaks red
as Cosimo's trickster stone.
Embers cool in currents
winding violet into deeper shades.

When you leave the Arno
pal, you're lost, looking
where you used to be.
Streets arc and widen.  Why
is the city so large? Il duomo,
broken, you're in too far.  Vermouth
gods in the plaza, speaking
in tongues.

Underground, you don't
know how, the passage
that eludes you, opens
like the old days.
Something in the curve
of the dark slipping away.


II.
Along hedges of cactus
and dune, footfalls fade
down trails of sand.
A minaret leans,
vault and dome wet
from shadow and moon.

Across the strait, another
ancient Roman city
sinks its shoulders in the sand.

III.

Out in the midday sun
    where I don't belong,
apparition in the glare.
The sea laps languid
    against the shore.
I am on my knees.
    I thirst.


When you come, I am.

RELIQUARY


The basilica passage takes
you down, from crypt to crypt
to a crypt below.  Yellow light
in the side chapels, sepulchres
smooth and pale.

A heretic is burning.  Wrong
turn where the guidebook
page is missing.  How little
we find one another.

A stele flames
in the plaza ruins.
Something in a
niche, lintel
and bone, fixes
your stare. You
can't move.  It is
screaming.

Holy blessed virgin mother of God.

Back through the plaza's
receding perspectival planes,
the bus is idling (don't
be a tourist) to take
you home.

MONROE DOCTRINE

From a list of Guatemalan disappeared:
Cortes Estrada, Ingrid Mariela, September 1980

The sprinkler ticks on a summer eve.
On the porch they gaze into the end of the day.
The barking of a dog fades into the streetlight's buzzing
    hum.
And as one listens, he thinks he hears
a sound that lies behind the shrubbery's drowsy leaves,
trace of a sound of someone screaming,

on the far side of night in Guatemala.

On the soft back lawn
the moon falls down upon her knees.
When the wind calms you can hear her,
Mariela, in liquid, melting veils,
whisper on the breath of the night air.

## THE FRONTIERS OF FISHING

The pick-up, fenders worn
gray silver, is alone on the road
between sleep and the metallic white
                                  of opening day.

"Your dad was quite a guy,"
Uncle Mike is saying.
The colors in the meadow on the right
flash wet.  Hawk into the trees.
He hands me the thermos to open.
"Smart, too. Knew where he was going."
Mike's breath comes out in steam.
Floorboard numb on the feet,
engine unhurried, sheepskin
warm on the shoulders, I fade.

I dream the frontiers of fishing,
wooden walk in the eastback woods,
men in high rubber boots, with gear and tackle,
intentions, whispers, and trades.

They are searching for the hidden lake,
beyond the ore cars and abandoned mine,
beyond the juniper scrub and high aspen
green white flash, beyond
the trail you lost this way before.

Look—suddenly it's there—
into the black waters rippling silver
soft along an invisible shore.
The glow of a firefly fades.

He wades into night,
feet sinking in the mud below,
pole half-floating in the dark close by.

ICICLE CHOIR

Icicles over the kitchen
window in choirs, like
organ pipes, or solitary,
wetten slowly.

Nebulas along
an expanding
curve burst,
then clear,
mirror. Liquid
crystal drops, the
ground below glazed,
glistening.

Frosted pane, sunglare,
midmorning (candle glow
eyelids moist and closing)

I gaze

Mountains melt in the distance

To you.

KAIROUAN

I.
Around the courtyard perimeter
the line of arches rises and falls.
Someone climbs the minaret's outside stairs
circling, slowing, in and out of view.
The sun on the central square is still.
Shadows fall back into arcades.

> The voice sounds along the halls,
> through colonnades, under vaults,
> unfolding in a soft cascade,
> as memory unfolds
> from within, as laughter,
> the glow of streetlight on a whitewashed wall,
> indistinct shapes of a palm grove at night,
> clouds passing over the stars,
> a ledge of tombs carved into the rock,
> opening into deepening darkness
> while water filters in below among the stone slabs
> and pools.

The last call fades,
the yard-stones warm to the feet.
The old wood door opens
onto the white blaze of day.


II.
Domes tilt and slide
billowing in the moonlight.
The flat roofs of apartments pass among them,
highways into night,
stone frame of the city
the color of bone.


III.
The East wind
     touches your hand to her hair.
Ambrosial darkness.   A breath
beside you lifts and falls.
Peace until the break of dawn.

THE OTHER WAY

There on the map
where the roads wander
and lose themselves
There on that white space
where the only direction is from
Friends and strangers
pass through me the other way
the old longing flowing through me

Sands open
The sea is still
beneath an unseen sun
Arches flash a wash of white
then curve into the bougainvillea's
scarlet flame
dust and velvet
You are met at the doorway
long expected
intimately known

# GRIEF WAS BETWEEN US

TRANSLATIONS FROM IBN 'ARABI'S
*TRANSLATOR OF DESIRES*

GAZELLES WHO SHOW YOU THE SUN

In Dhu Sálam and at
the monastery in al-Híma
are gazelles who show you
the sun as marbled figurines.

I observe the spheres,
serve a basilica
and guard a garden
jeweled with spring.

Gazelle-herder
of the empty regions
they call me,
monk, astrologer.

The one I love is three
though one,
like the three persons, they proclaim,
in a single being.

Don't contradict my word,
friend, about Sun Gaze
lighting the way for gazelles
as they circle the figurines—

Necks of the fawn,
faces of the sun,
a blood-marbled statue
with a wrist and breast.

As we lend garments
to the branches of a tree,
virtues to a garden,
and to the lightning a smile.

## GRIEF WAS BETWEEN US

The ringnecked dove cooed.
A sad man yearned,
disquieted
by the echo of her longing.

At the sound of her desire,
eyes welled,
sudden as underground springs
bursting.

She mourned her
only one. I responded.
Loss is the loss
of your one and only.

I called back a cry
but grief was between us.
I revealed myself.
She stayed hidden.

I felt love's sting
on the sands of 'Alij
white tents along the slopes,
the large-of-eyes,

gaze languid,
glances fatal,
eyelids sheathes
of swords that glisten.

I choked back tears
from what was hurting me,
hiding my love from the blame-monger,
acting well.

Until the crow cawed
time to leave, time for separation
and exposed the love run wild
of a man who grieves.

The riders reached, cutting
the nose-rings of their camels,

red roans beneath the saddle,
moaning, yearning.

Before my eyes
I saw the cords of fated death,
as they loosened the reins
and cinched the strap of the saddle.

In the fever of love,
separation kills.
Finding her
would ease the burning.

No one blames me
wanting her.
I love her
beauty wherever she turns.

## THE HADITH OF LOVE

He saw the lightning flash
and yearned toward the East.
If it had flashed West
west he'd have turned.

I burn for the lightning,
for the flash,
not for this or that—
some piece of ground.

The East wind told me
a tradition about them, from
the wreck of my heart, from
ecstasy, sorrow, my disarray

From drunkenness, reason,
longing, the wound of love,
from tears, my eyelids,
the fire, my heart:

He whom you desire
is between your ribs,
turned side to side
in the heat of your sigh.

I told them tell him
he's the one
who kindled the fire
blazing in my heart.

It is extinguished only
in our coming together. If
it burns out of control,
who can be blamed for loving?

## IN BETWEEN FLATTENED ON THE GROUND

They left me in Atháyl
        and in Náqa
pouring out tears,
        complaining of fire.

                By the life of my father!
        In whom did I sorrow?
                By the life of my father!
        In whom did I die leaving?

On his cheek the red sign
        of not knowing what to do,
the light of morning
        whispering in the glow of dusk.

        The tent of patience is down.
                Sorrow has raised camp.
        I'm in between
                flattened on the ground.

Who is here for me undone,
        for my ecstasy, guide me!
for my sadness, for a love
        gone mad.

        I tried to hide
the burn wounds of loving.
        Red-eyed tears and sleepless night
gave my grief away.

If I ask for just a look,
        they say:
we only hold you back
        in compassion.

        A look cannot set you free
of them ever.
        It's only a flash
crackling the sky.

I'll never forget the sight,
        the camel driver

urging them down the track
    seeking the parting of ways in Al-Ábraq.


    Gone, gone,
cawed the crows of separation,
    God leave rotting on the path
a crow that caws!


And what are the crows of separation
    but camel stallions
pacing hard,
    taking those we love away.

YOU WHO PASTURE THE STARS

They placed their howdahs
on long-stride camels,
full moons within the curtains,
and marbled figurines.

They promised my heart
they would return.  What is
the promise of a young beauty
but delusion.

They beckoned goodbye,
fingertips dyed henna.
They set tears scattering,
stoked a fire.

They turned
back toward Yemen,
seeking Khawárnaq
   then Sadír.

Damn it! I called
as they left.
They answered
If you want to cry damn it,

Why settle for
a single, lonely damnation?
Damn it, damn it,
    Damn it all over!

    Easy now,
    dove of the thornberry thicket,
    her leaving
    has sharpened your cry.

Your coo, dove,
incites the lover
and inflames one
    already burning,

Melts the heart,
turns sleep away,

compounds our longing
   and our sigh.

Death hovers
over a dove that coos.
We beg of him
   a stay.

   Perhaps a breath
   from the East wind,
   from Hájir,
   will bring us clouds of rain.

You who pasture the stars
be my drinking companion!
And you, lightning gazer with the sleepless eye,
   my friend through the night!

   And you who prefer
   to sleep the night away,
   before you die, already
   you inhabit the tomb.

If only you had loved
a  bravesouled beauty,
you'd have found in her what you desired
        and been satisfied.

    You'd be sharing with the belles
    intimate wine, speaking
    secrets to the sun, and to the moon
        whispering nothings.

GOD CURSE MY LOVE


O you who drive the red roans,
don't drive them further.  Pause.
I drag myself along after,
        falling behind.

Rein the camels in.
Loose the bridles.  By God!
By the trance of desire!
        By what hurts so bad!  Driver!

My soul wants
what my limbs can't bear.
Who can offer me some support,
        some consolation?

When the craftsman
skilled in his trade,
finds his tools fail him,
        what can he fashion?

Turn aside.  Their tents
are in the wádi, on the right slope.
God bless you for what you hold,
    wádi!

You embrace a people
who are my soul,
my breath, the darkest dark
    of the membrane of my liver.

God curse my love
if I don't die grieving
at Hájir or at Sal'
    or in Ajyádi.

AS COOL AS LIFE

At the way stations
    stay.  Grieve over the ruins.
Ask the meadow grounds,
    desolate, this question:

    Where are those we loved,
    where have their red roans gone?
    Over there,
    cutting through the desert haze.

Like gardens in a mirage,
    you see them,
their silhouettes enlarged
    in the diaphanous mists.

    They have gone off seeking
Al-'Udhayb,
    to drink its waters
as cool as life.

I tracked after them.
 I asked the East wind.
Have they set up tents
 or sheltered within the Lote Tree's shade?

  She said:  I left their camp
   on the sand-tossed plain of Zarúd,
  the camels, wearied from the long night's journey,
   complaining.

They let a curtain down
 over their pavilions
to shelter beauty
 from the mid-day heat.

  Get up your camels
 and set off seeking
  their traces, amber camels
 pacing toward them.

When you stop
 before the way-marks of Hájir

and cut across its ridges
and hollows,

Their stations will be near.
Their fire will loom before you,
kindling desire
into a raging blaze.

Kneel your camels there.
Don't fear their lions.
Longing will reveal them to you
newborn cubs.

## THE TOMBS OF THOSE WHO LOVED THEM

O windswept wasted ruin at al-Utháyl,
    where I used to play
        with young women
who knew discretion.

Yesterday it embraced us
    laughing. Today
        it frowns
in desolation.

They left without
    my knowing.
        Little did they know
my inner self could see

and follow, however far
    they journeyed, wherever
        they set their tents.
It might have been I leading their camels.

Until they halted
    in the barrenlands,
        pitched their tents
and spread their carpets.

They were brought back to a garden,
    wet colors singing,
        on what had been drought-split
hardened empty ground.

Whatever halt they chose
    to take their rest
        was filled with forms of beauty
like peacocks.

When they struck camp
    they left a land
        holding the tombs
of those who loved them.

YOUR WISH OF TANGLED SHADE

O meadowed slope of the riverbed,
answer the lady lord of this sacral ground,
her with the wet flash from her side teeth,
    meadow of the wádi!

        Offer her a little shade
        for awhile, until one
        who calls to meet her
            rests by her side.

Within your desert reaches
she has pitched her tent,
with all the dew you wish
    to nourish branches as they sway,

        Your wish of rain,
        gift of the clouds, flowing
        over blossoms of moringa
            morning and evening,

Your wish of tangled shade,
and fruits of every kind
swaying, bending low
    for one who gathers.

        Your wish of those seeking
        the moistened sands of Zarúd,
        pushed on by chanting drivers
            and led by chanting guides.

MY GUTS ARE PLUNDERED. I'VE LOST.


Woe, my guts are plundered
and oh my soul's enthralled!

Within me fire burns. The full moon
of the night sky sets in my soul.

Musk, full moon, branch on the whitened dune
flowering into light, the fragrance!

Wet lips of the smile I love,
nectar of the mouth I knew,

Pale moon apparition on the cheek
veiled in the disarray of love.

If he had lowered his veil, he'd have
put me to the torture. He let it be.

Midday sun rising in its heaven,

bough of a grassy dune transplanted into garden,

I kept watch, apprehensive,
watering that branch with a bursting sky.

She rose and cast a spell on my eyes.
She set and set me dying.

Beauty laced the strands of her hair
in a tiara of gold.  I caught gold fever.

If Iblís had seen the light of her face on Adam
he would not have refused to worship.

If Idrís had seen on her cheekbone the talisman of
    beauty
wisdom's sage would have turned in his pen.

If Bilqís had seen her tapestry, Solomon's throne
and towering hall would have slipped her mind.

Sarh tree of the riverbed, moringa of the tamarisk grove

send us your fragrance on the East wind,

Waft of musk, exhalation of the blossoms
of the lowlands and the blossoms of the hills,

Moringa of the riverbed, show me a bough
or a wreath bouquet soft as her shoulder.

The East wind tells of a time made young
at Hájir, Mína, or Qúba,

At the dune, at the bend of the path, near the sacred
     precinct,
or at La'la' where gazelles browse.

No wonder no wonder no wonder at all
an Arab trades desire with a belle of the sands.

He passes away at the warbled cry
of the turtledove calling back the one he loves.

GONE SAD

Red-roan driver, turn aside at Sál'in
Halt by the moringa tree at Mudárraj

Call to them gently, with politesse,
        Mesdames, can you give me comfort?

At Ráma between White Sands and Hájir
        there is a shy-eyed girl in a howdah,

Child beauty who lights the way,
        like a lamp
for a man who walks the night,

Pearl in a shell of hair as black as jet,

Your mind dives to reach it
never to emerge from the watery deep.

Neck supple, gestures coquette
bring to mind a gazelle of the sandy hills,

Like the forenoon sun
    in the constellation Aries
cutting across the cosmic reaches.

When she takes down her veil
when she shows her face
    she veils the morning
    light with her shadow.

I called to her between Híma and Ráma:

Who is here for a braveheart
    who halts at Sál'in and hopes
Who for a braveheart
    lost in the hollow desert,
    love-burned, love-mad, gone sad
Who for a braveheart
    drowned in his tears,
    drunk from the wine
        of her open mouth

Who for a braveheart
    burned by his own sighs,
    led astray and abandoned
    in the beauty of the glow between her eyes.

The hands of desire
    played on his heart.
What is there to hold against him?
    Where is his crime?

## ON THE BED DONE IN

Traitoress with curls twisted like snakes!
She leaves behind a man who sought

the straight path.  She coiled her glistening softness,
melted him away and left him

on the bed, done in.  From whatever side
I come, I'm gone.

STAY NOW AT THE RUINS FADING

*Ibn 'Arabi said: An ascetic recited for me a verse the like of which I had never heard. The verse was:*

*Everyone who wanted you,*
*you showered with graces.*
*Only to me did your lightning*
*flash, unfaithful.*

*Its power amazed me and I tracked after its meaning. I composed verses in this rhyme, including the original verse in full, as a response to that ascetic, may God Almighty rest his soul. He [Ibn 'Arabi] said:*

Stay now at the ruins
in Lá'la'i, fading,
and in that wasteland, grieve,
for those we loved.

At the campsite, now abandoned,
stay and call her name,
as your heart is softly
torn away,

For the time of one like me
spent near her moringa's gossamer flowering,
plucking at fruits, in measure,
and at the petals of a rose, red, ripening.

Everyone who wanted you,
you showered with graces.
Only to me did your lightning
flash, unfaithful.

Yes, she said,
there we used to come together,
in the shade of my branches,
in that luxuriant land.

My lightning
was the flash of smiles,

Now it is the blaze
of barren stone.

So blame that time
we had no way of warding off.
What fault was it
of Láʻlaʻi?

I forgave her
as I heard her speak,
grieving as I grieved
with a wounded heart.

I asked her—
when I saw her meadows
now fields of the four
scouring, twisting winds—

Did they tell you where
they'd take their noonday rest?
Yes, she said,
at Sand Hill,

Where the white tents gleam
with what they hold—
from all those rising
suns—of splendor.

# GLOSSARY

Note: terms are listed first with stress accent, followed by transliteration with quantitative markings.

Pronunciation of long vowels:
ā (can be pronounced either like "au" in caught or the "a" in cat),
ī (like the "ee" in keen),
ū (like the "oo" in noon)

'Árafat *('arafāt)*.  The plain near Mecca where Muhammad gave his last sermon and where hajj pilgrims stand for a full day in remembrance of that event.  At this time, the pilgrims also chant "*labbayka*" (here I am for you), the expression each person will utter at the final judgment.

atlál *(atlāl)*.  The ruin of the abandoned campsite of the beloved over which the poet and lover persona meditates and conceives the love poem.

Eis *('īs)*. One of hundreds of precise epithets for the camel used by the bedouin. In this case it refers to roan camels of a sandy or reddish tint.

Isa, Eissa *('īsā)*. The Arabic form of Jesus, the Qur'anic prophet with whom Ibn 'Arabi felt particular affinity.

Bilqís (bilqīs). The queen of Sheba associated in the Qur'an with the splendor of her court and the acuteness of her intellect. She is outdueled in a contest with Solomon when, standing in Solomon's Temple, she lifts her skirts as if she were in a pool, deceived by the shimmering brilliance of the tiles.

dúma *(dumā)*. Statuettes or figurines, made of alabaster or veined marble and used by Syrian Christians, and the object of intense interest to Ibn 'Arabi as a symbol for the unmoved beloved who is as unresponsive to questions and pleas as the old hearth stones of the beloved's abandoned campsite addressed by the pre-Islamic poets.

East wind, Sába *(ṣabā)*. The messenger between the beloved and lover, the bearer of the fragrance of the beloved's memory and of the promise of spring, sometimes standing in for the beloved in dialogues with the lover.

Gháda (*ghaḍā*). A grove in Arabia associated with the romance world of Majnūn Laylā.

Hájir (*ḥājir*). A place name based on the word for rock or stone, an alternative name for *Madā'in Ṣāliḥ*, the ancient city in Central Arabia, probably of the same Nabataen civilization as Petra. The ruins of the city enchanted the bedouin and touched them with a sense of the ominous. In the Qur'anic story, the city was destroyed when its people refused to follow the advice of their prophet Salih and carried out a sacrilegious slaughter of the camel mare of God (*nāqat allāh*). Ibn 'Arabi speaks of the East wind life breath from Hājir, a paradox with allusions to the Sufi doctrine of mystical annihilation in union with the beloved.

hówdah (*hawdaj*). A frame enclosure placed upon camels as a litter, in which women could travel sheltered from heat, glare, and the gaze of men.

háram *(al-ḥaram)*. Sacred place or sacred time. The sacrality of place is tied to the prohibitions on entering it improperly. The Kaʻba in Mecca is considered the first *ḥaram* of Islam (and was considered a *ḥaram* in pre-Islamic Arabia as well). It can be entered only with ritual purification. All violence in the area is forbidden. The one aspect of the term familiar in the West refers to the women's quarters of a family dwelling. *Ḥaram* refers to that which has the quality of being *ḥarām*, especially in the sense of being forbidden. Thus wine, pork, and all food attained by improperly gained wealth are *ḥaram*.

Híma, al-Híma *(al-ḥimā)*. The sacred tribal enclosure in bedouin Arabia, marked with boundary stones, the transgression of which by another tribe would lead automatically to war. In Ibn ʻArabi's poems, *al-ḥimā* is the name of one of the stations of the beloved (and of the lover following her tracks). Ibn ʻArabi employs the term in such a way that it can be either a common name or a proper name: Sanctuary or the sanctuary.

Iblís (*iblīs*). The fallen angel. In the Qur'anic creation accounts, God ordered the angels to bow before Adam. One of them, Iblis, refused and was cast out of the heavens to become the Satan figure, tempting the offspring of his ancient rival Adam. Some writers suggest Iblis could not have been a true angel, but was a genie instead.

Idrís (*idrīs*). Idrīs is a Qur'anic prophet associated with the Biblical Enoch and, in later writings, with Hermes. Idrīs represents wisdom, esoteric sciences, and in the symbolic universe based on Ptolemaic spheres, the sphere of the Sun.

jinn or genies (*jinn*, singular *jinnī*). Semi-spirits of the desert associated in the ancient poetry with love, madness, and poetic inspiration. They frequently appeared to the poet in the desert, transforming themselves through various guises.

Khawarnaq and Sadír (*khawarnaq* and *sadīr*). Ruins of ancient civilizations of southeast Iraq, legendary ruins in the case of Sadír, ruins of a more recent historical time in the case of Khawarnaq. The two names became proverbial signs of the ineluctable force of time that wears away even the grandest monuments of humankind.

khayál, tayf *(khayāl, ṭayf)*. The apparition of the beloved to the poet, an apparition that can fill the same role in the beginning of a *nasīb* as the ruin of the beloved's campsite. It is worth noting that the deeper, archaic meaning of *khayāl*, which later comes to mean imagination, is the apparition of the beloved.

Lá‘la‘ *(la‘la‘)*. Stone-Flash, one of many toponoyms built upon natural features, along the lines of the American names Flint-Rock, Rock-Creek, Flint-Creek. In the poetry, the etymological grounding of the term is revived. Lá‘la‘ is a place name associated with the stations of the beloved and with the tradition of Majnūn Laylā.

Láyla *(laylā)*. The beloved in the poems attributed to Qays ibn Mulawwih, the semi-legendary bedouin poet said to have lived at the time of the prophet

Muhammad. In the poems attributed to him, and in the Romances about him (in Arabic, Persian, Ottoman, and other languages), Qays is said to have gone insane out of his unrequited love for Layla, to have wandered aimlessly (*hā'im*) through the desert, and to have suffered final destruction (*halāk*) in his love for her. Thus he became known as Majnūn Laylā (Mad for Layla). The epithet *majnūn* (mad) carried the etymological sense of "jinned."

Lote Tree (*dāl*). The tree that serves as *locus amoenis*, the mark of a love remembered or of poetic vision. In the religion of love it is the analogue to the other species of lote tree (*sidr*) upon which Muhammad saw the prophetic vision.

Máyya (*mayya*). The beloved in the poems of Ghaylan ibn 'Uqba, also known as Dhu r-Rumma, who flourished in the Umayyad period and whose qasidas, dominated by *nasīb* motifs, served as a model for Ibn 'Arabi in both the *adab* (comportment) of the lover and the style of poetic composition.

Mína *(minā).* The station of the hajj where pilgrims cast stones at pillars representing evil tendencies or Satan, and where sheep, goats, or camels are sacrificed in memory of Abraham's offering made in place of his son. The sacrifice is carried out on the great 'Id (Aid), the major feast day in Islam, and at the same time Muslims around the world perform a sacrifice in solidarity with the pilgrims and in remembrance of Abraham.

Najd *(najd).* The eastern highland plateau of Arabia, associated with the world of love poetry, Majnun Layla, and the East wind. Najd is frequently contrasted to Tihām, the lowland area along the western shore of Arabia.

Na'mán *(na'mān).* A station of ambiguous geographical placement associated with the tradition of Majnūn Laylā. The etymology of Na'mān would suggest American toponyms such as Bountiful, Springfield, or Pleasant Grove.

Namús *(an-nāmūs)*. An enigmatic figure in Arabic poetry. The clearest etymology connects it to the Greek *nomos* (law) and to revelation as law. The word also comes to mean a great spirit and is sometimes said to be an epithet of Gabriel. In Arab Christianity the term refers to the spirit that descends upon the apostles at Pentecost.

Nasíb *(nasīb)*. The amatory first section of the classical Arabic ode or qasida. It is commonly introduced through the meditation over the ruins of the beloved's campsite. Those meditations lead in turn to the remembrance of being with her, the remembrance of separation from her, and reveries concerning the beloved and the symbolic analogue of the beloved, the lost garden.

Nizám *(niẓām)*. Sometimes referred to as Ibn 'Arabi's Beatrice. Daughter of a Persian shaykh who had settled in Mecca and niece of a renowned female scholar with whom Ibn 'Arabi had wished to study. Ibn 'Arabi relates that his encounter with Niẓām at the Ka'ba led to the composition of the *Turjumān*. The word *niẓām* means harmony, harmonious order, and harmonious cadence and, more concretely, the order of pearls or other artistic objects.

Sun Gaze (*ghazāla*). This relatively rare word is an epithet for the sun that is etymologically related to *ghazal* (love-talk, erotic poetry), and *ghazāl* (gazelle).

Stoning Ground. The Stoning Ground is an area at Mina at which hajj pilgrims ritually cast pebbles at pillars said to represent evil tendencies or the devil.

Thornberry (*arāk*) and Moringa (*bān*). The *arāk* is a thorny desert shrub the twigs of which were used by bedouin as toothpicks. The moringa is a beautiful small tree with delicate curling blossoms. The *arāk* twig evoked associations with the beloved's mouth, a key signal for erotic digression in Arabic poetry. The moringa evoked associations with the beloved's hair. Both plants are native to the Arabian desert and their mention in a poem immediately brings to mind the Arabian context.

Za'n (*za'n*).  A term from the bedouin nasib indicating the departure of the women of the tribe, their mounting into the camel howdahs, and their movement away from the campsite.  The scene, if not the term itself, is utilized throughout Ibn 'Arabi's *Turjumān*.

Zámzam (*zamzam*):  The spring of miraculous water near the Ka'ba that tradition holds was opened by God in response to Hagar's desperate search for water.